CM PUNK

STRAIGHT EDGE HEEL

by Jennifer Fandel

Consultant:
Mike Johnson, Writer
PWInsider.com

CAPSTONE PRESS
a capstone imprint

Velocity is published by Capstone Press,
1710 Roe Crest Drive, North Mankato, Minnesota 56003.
www.capstonepress.com

Library of Congress Cataloging-in-Publication Data
Fandel, Jennifer.
    CM Punk: straight edge heel / by Jennifer Fandel.
    p. cm.—(Velocity. Pro wrestling stars.)
    Includes bibliographical references and index.
    Summary: "Describes the life of CM Punk, both in and out of the ring"—Provided by
publisher.
    ISBN 978-1-4296-8693-8 (library binding)
    ISBN 978-1-62065-358-6 (ebook pdf)
    1. CM Punk, 1978—Juvenile literature. 2. Wrestlers—United States—Biography—
Juvenile literature. I. Title.
GV1196.C25F36 2012
796.812092—dc23 [B]   2012011286

Editorial Credits
Mandy Robbins, editor; Sarah Bennett, designer; Laura Manthe, production specialist

Photo Credits
Alamy: ZUMA Wire Service, 29; AP Images for WWE: Jim R. Bounds, 15, El Nuevo Dia/
Reinhold Matay, 38, Starpix/Dave Allocca, 45; Getty Images: Mark Metcalfe, 43; iStockphotos:
grimgram, 37; Newscom: SIPA/Revelli-Beaumont, 30, WENN Photos CD1, 8-9, WENN
Photos SI1, cover, ZUMA Press, 5, 12, 17, 19, 24, 33, 35, 36; Photo by Wrealano@aol.
com, 20; Shutterstock: Dmitry Kalinovsky, 10 (jujitsu), Ffooter, 6 (fence), Galushko Sergey,
44, Genotar, 6 (buildings), Helga Esteb, 7, Hluboki Dzianis, 18 (footprints), ilolab, 36-37
(map background), James Steidl, 39, karlovserg, 21 (handcuffs), komar_off, 16, konahinab,
26, 27 (winged frames), Panacea_Doll, 10-11 (map), photofriday, 11 (Thai fighters),
Pinnacleanimates, 19 (trophy), Rudy Balasko, 26-27 (city background), Shamzami, 42;
Wikimedia: David Seto, 31, Fatima, cover, 1 (background), Feedback, 27 (CM Punk), 41,
jorgebueno, 34, LINXBAS, 13, Mshake3, 23, 26 (Ace Steel), Randy Chancellor, 32, Raven,
21, Vishal Somaiya, 25, Cameraman Greg, 27 (Colt Cabana)

Artistic Effects
Shutterstock

Printed in the United States of America in Stevens Point, Wisconsin.
032012   006678WZF12

TABLE OF CONTENTS

SECOND CITY SAVIOR

In CM Punk's short pro wrestling career, he has quickly become one of the hottest stars in World Wrestling Entertainment (WWE). He is known as the Second City Savior and the Straight Edge Superstar. Punk has won the WWE Championship and the WWE World Heavyweight Championship. He has also taken home the World Tag Team Championship, the Intercontinental Championship, and the Triple Crown. Punk is the only wrestler to win **MONEY IN THE BANK** two years in a row. Since he signed on with the WWE in 2005, Punk has steadily worked his way to the top. And that's where he wants to stay.

FACT

Chicago, Illinois, is called the Second City because it burned to the ground in 1871. It was rebuilt bigger and better than ever.

When a wrestler reaches the top of the ladder in a Money in the Bank ladder match, he wins a chance at a world title match. The wrestler can "cash it in" at any time. This means he can challenge a current title holder to wrestle for that title and the title holder can't refuse.

CM Punk won Money in the Bank for the first time at *WrestleMania* on March 30, 2008.

CHAPTER 1

BECOMING A PUNK

CM Punk's real name is Phillip Jack Brooks. He was born and raised in Chicago, Illinois. When he was a teenager, Phillip wrestled in backyard wrestling leagues. Even back then, he called himself "Punk." One day, someone didn't show up for a **tag team** match, and Punk jumped into the ring. Everyone on the team used CM in their names. It stood for "chick magnet." That was the day Punk became CM Punk. The name stuck.

Punk wrestled in backyard wrestling leagues for the rest of high school. After high school, he trained at the Steel Domain Wrestling school in Chicago. In 1999 he wrestled in his first **independent wrestling league**, and he was hooked. Punk went on to wrestle for different wrestling leagues around the United States. He was on the road a lot, wrestling almost every night of the week. Punk loved every minute of it.

tag team—when two or more wrestlers partner together against other teams

independent wrestling league—a small wrestling group that competes outside of the WWE

WHAT'S IN A NAME?

A lot of people ask CM Punk what the "CM" stands for. Sometimes he tells people that CM stands for Cookie Monster. Punk likes to play around when people focus on his name. He doesn't take the initials seriously, but he thinks they sound good with Punk.

TIMELINE OF A CHAMPION

CM Punk has wrestled professionally for more than 10 years. He's made his way to the top championship by championship.

CM PUNK

HEIGHT
6 feet, 2 inches
(188 centimeters)

WEIGHT
218 pounds (99 kilograms)

SIGNATURE MOVES
Anaconda Vise, G.T.S.

2002
Punk made his **debut** with the independent wrestling league Ring of Honor (ROH).

2000
Punk started wrestling in independent wrestling leagues to build up his skills.

2005
Punk won the ROH World Championship. Later that year, he made the big step of entering WWE's developmental system.

2007
Punk became the ECW World Champion.

2006
Punk made his WWE Extreme Championship Wrestling (ECW) debut.

2008
Punk won the WWE World Heavyweight Championship for the first time. He also won the World Tag Team title with Kofi Kingston.

2009
Punk won the Intercontinental Championship and became a WWE **TRIPLE CROWN** Champion.

TRIPLE CROWN

The Triple Crown Champion is the name given to someone who has won three titles. The main WWE titles are the WWE Championship, the WWE World Heavyweight Championship, the World Tag Team Championship, and the Intercontinental Championship. The national wrestling leagues Ring of Honor (ROH) and Total Nonstop Action Wrestling (TNA) also award the Triple Crown.

2011
Punk won the WWE Championship.

debut—a first public appearance

CHAPTER 2
PUNK MOVES

PUNK'S TRAVELS

Punk enjoys traveling and has been to Europe, Asia, and Central and South America. On his travels, he picked up **JUJITSU** moves from Brazil and **MUAY THAI** moves from Thailand.

Most of CM Punk's matches have taken place in North America. But he does travel to London, England, for matches from time to time. He has wrestled twice in Baghdad, Iraq, for the American military troops stationed there.

BRAZIL

JUJITSU is sometimes called "the gentle art." Buddhist monks in India developed it. The techniques eventually ended up in Brazil. Jujitsu is about using the body's balance as a weapon. Strength alone isn't important in jujitsu.

CM Punk has fans all over the world. He is popular in Japan and many European countries. These fans usually can only see CM Punk on TV. It's a big treat when he travels to sign autographs and meet his fans from all over the world.

● **MUAY THAI** is Thailand's national sport. The hand-to-hand combat skills were used by the Thai army long ago. Muay Thai is about using power and speed to knock out your opponent. It's now very popular among kickboxers.

FINISH 'EM

Punk has combined jujitsu and Muay Thai moves with more common pro wrestling moves. He has also added a style and flair that makes his moves uniquely Punk.

ANACONDA VISE

This **submission hold** is one of Punk's **finishing moves**. It is taken from Brazilian jujitsu. The Anaconda Vise is a dangerous choke hold. To do this move, CM Punk uses his opponent's arm to create the choke. He wraps the arm around his opponent's neck. He holds it there with his own hands.

SPRINGBOARD FLYING CLOTHESLINE

One of CM Punk's most exciting moves is the Springboard Flying Clothesline. This move requires great balance because it's done from the ropes. CM Punk stands on the mat outside of the ropes, and then he leaps up to the top rope. Punk hovers there for a moment and then launches himself toward his opponent. He jumps with his arm outstretched so that it smacks into the other wrestler's neck, slamming him to the floor.

G.T.S.

The G.T.S. is CM Punk's most popular finishing move. It stands for "Go to Sleep." He starts with a fireman's carry. In this lift, the opponent is picked up at the knees and tossed over CM Punk's shoulders. Then Punk drops his opponent in front of him. When the opponent is on the way down, CM Punk raises his knee to strike him in the face.

submission hold—a chokehold, joint hold, or compression lock that causes a fighter's opponent to end the match by tapping out or saying, "I submit"

finishing move—the move for which a wrestler is best known; this move also is called a signature move

CHAPTER 3
PUNK STYLE, PUNK BELIEFS

CM Punk's motto is "Luck is for losers." Punk believes people create their own luck by working and training hard. Sometimes people get lucky. But Punk wants people to realize that luck isn't everything. If you're not prepared to succeed, luck won't help you at all.

GOALS

In Punk's case, he was a skinny kid with a dream. He set goals and steadily worked toward them. His first big goal was to wrestle in the WWE. After that, he wanted to become a champion—a Triple Crown Champion! No goal was too big for CM Punk.

COSTUMES

Punk's costumes are simple trunks paired with knee-high boots. When he first came to the WWE, he brought his own costumes. He knew that WWE was his chance to make it big. But he liked his style and hoped that he wouldn't have to change it for the WWE. He thought that if he came with his own costumes, the WWE might accept him just as he was. And they did!

Despite his motto, Punk covers himself in tattoos that are symbols of luck, such as dice and clovers. He says that he does this to make his fans look beyond appearances. Does he win because he's lucky? Of course not! He is driven to train hard and set new goals.

STRAIGHT EDGE

Not all of Punk's tattoos refer to luck. CM Punk's other tattoos come with a clear message. They are just one way that he speaks out against **peer pressure**.

FACT
The term "Straight Edge Movement" comes from the 1981 song "Straight Edge" by the punk band Minor Threat. CM Punk joined the movement when he was 15.

CM Punk's tattoo on his stomach reads "Straight Edge." CM Punk is a champion of the Straight Edge Movement. He doesn't think people should do anything that hurts or weakens the brain or body. This includes smoking cigarettes, drinking alcohol, and using illegal drugs.

Punk doesn't drink alcohol. He tells people "I like Pepsi."

peer pressure—pressure from one's friends trying to get a person to do something he or she thinks is wrong

Some people make fun of Punk for being smaller than other pro wrestlers. He says that his muscles are all natural. He's simply built smaller than other pro wrestlers. Punk doesn't use **steroids**, as some wrestlers have done in the past.

Punk often wears bandages with an "X" over his hands. The "X" is a symbol for people who follow the Straight Edge Movement. It's another way to show his support for the movement.

Punk has "Drug Free" tattooed on his knuckles.

STEROIDS

Many sports have received negative attention for players caught using steroids. Steroids are drugs that can make a person's muscles stronger and bigger in a short amount of time. But there are bad side effects. The drugs can affect the way a person thinks, making him or her easily angry. People may also grow more hair or get pimples. Steroids can even harm the body. They increase a person's chance of getting cancer. Today steroid use is against the rules in pro wrestling.

steroid—an illegal drug that can increase a person's strength and athletic ability; steroids can cause heart problems and death

A HEEL ABOVE THE REST

CM Punk isn't your typical **heel**. Heels are supposed to be bad to the bone. Everyone knows to boo the heel and cheer for the **babyface**. But can a heel be good?

CM Punk's Straight Edge message is positive, and many young fans have followed in his footsteps. But Punk believes in breaking the rules to spread his message and get attention. He doesn't spare anyone's feelings, and he will turn on anyone who doesn't believe as he does. He thinks that the pain he brings opponents isn't half as bad as the pain they bring themselves if they use illegal drugs and drink alcohol.

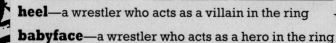

heel—a wrestler who acts as a villain in the ring

babyface—a wrestler who acts as a hero in the ring

CM Punk gives Chris Jericho a kick to the chin during a 2008 match.

SLAMMY AWARDS

Slammy Awards are like the Oscars of pro wrestling. There are awards like "Best Moment" and "Shocker of the Year." But there are also awards that make fun of the wrestlers, like "Knucklehead of the Year" and "Meltdown of the Year." In 2008 Punk won a Slammy Award for the "OMG Moment of the Year." He won the award for defeating Jeff Hardy just minutes after Hardy claimed the World Heavyweight Championship.

CHAPTER 4
FIERCE FEUDS

Over the years, Punk's bad attitude has gotten him into a number of feuds. He uses each rivalry as a chance to spread his positive message.

PUNK VS. RAVEN

CM Punk's first big rivalry was with Raven. It lasted almost a year. Their first match was at ROH's *Expect the Unexpected* in 2003. CM Punk spoke out against Raven and his use of alcohol. CM Punk won the match, but he wouldn't shake Raven's hand. He surprised him with a punch instead.

CM Punk and Raven often fought brutal **STEEL CAGE** matches. Sometimes they fought in matches that Raven created, such as the **"CLOCKWORK ORANGE HOUSE OF FUN"** match. Some of their matches were fought as tag teams. CM Punk often paired up with Colt Cabana and Julio Dinero. Punk won most of the matches. He thought it proved that avoiding drugs and alcohol made him a stronger person than Raven.

Raven has been in many steel cage matches during his time at ROH.

STEEL CAGE MATCH

In a steel cage match, the wrestling ring is surrounded by a steel cage. A wrestler can win the match by pinning an opponent on his back, forcing him to submit, or escaping the cage.

"CLOCKWORK ORANGE HOUSE OF FUN"

In this steel cage match, Punk and Raven faced off with weapons. The weapons included trash cans, steel chairs, chains, and even a shovel. At one point Punk had Raven handcuffed to the ring while he pounded on him. Raven freed himself, though. Eventually, he pinned Punk after both men slammed through a table.

RAVEN

HEIGHT
6 ft, 1 in (185 cm)

WEIGHT
244 lbs (111 kg)

SIGNATURE MOVE
Raven Effect

PUNK VS. JOHN MORRISON

In Extreme Championship Wrestling (ECW), CM Punk had a long-standing feud with John Morrison. Morrison also went by the name Johnny Nitro until July 2007. Morrison was the top heel in ECW. CM Punk defeated Morrison for the ECW Heavyweight Championship in 2007, but their battles continued. They faced off in more than 50 matches through 2011.

JOHN MORRISON

HEIGHT
6 ft (183 cm)

WEIGHT
215 lbs (98 kg)

SIGNATURE MOVES
Starship Pain, The Moonlight Drive

NOVEMBER 26, 2006

On November 26, 2006, CM Punk and Johnny Nitro faced off for the first time at WWE *Survivor Series*. Punk fought as part of Team DX, which included Triple H, Shawn Michaels, Jeff Hardy, and Matt Hardy. Team DX won against Johnny Nitro's team, Rated-RKO.

JUNE 24, 2007

On June 24, 2007, Johnny Nitro and CM Punk battled for the ECW World Championship title. CM Punk lost. In July and August, they squared off again for the title. CM Punk lost again.

SEPTEMBER 1, 2007

SEPTEMBER 1, 2007

On September 1, 2007, CM Punk finally took the ECW World Championship from John Morrison. It was a rough match that left fans on the edges of their seats. CM Punk was nearly pinned over and over again, but he got up each time with just a second to spare. At the very end, a few well-timed moves gave him the advantage over Morrison.

NOVEMBER 18, 2007

On November 18, 2007, CM Punk defended the World Championship title against both John Morrison and The Miz at *Survivor Series*.

Morrison flaunted his Tag Team Championship belt for fans before a match in Rosemont, Illinois.

FACT

ECW was an independent wrestling league in the 1990s. WWE purchased the company in 2001. CM Punk wrestled for ECW when he first joined the WWE.

In 2009 CM Punk fought hard to keep the WWE World Heavyweight Championship. He faced rough and tough rivals. Among them were Jeff Hardy and Undertaker.

PUNK VS. JEFF HARDY

On June 7, 2009, Jeff Hardy won his very first World Heavyweight Championship. Moments after Hardy's win, Punk cashed in his "Money in the Bank." Hardy was exhausted from the previous match. It wasn't hard for Punk to snatch the title away from him.

Jeff Hardy won the title back on June 28, but not for long. He lost the title twice to CM Punk in August. After the final loss, Hardy was forced to leave the WWE for good.

JEFF HARDY

HEIGHT
6 ft, 2 in (188 cm)

WEIGHT
215 lbs (98 kg)

SIGNATURE MOVE
Swanton Bomb

CM Punk shoved Undertaker into a casket during a Casket Match on August 11, 2009.

PUNK
VS.
UNDERTAKER

UNDERTAKER

HEIGHT
6 ft, 10 in (208 cm)

WEIGHT
299 lbs (136 kg)

SIGNATURE MOVES
Chokeslam, Tombstone Piledriver, and Last Ride

Once Jeff Hardy was out of the picture, CM Punk faced a challenge for the title from Undertaker. Punk kept the title in their first World Heavyweight Championship face-off in September 2009. But Undertaker wouldn't quit until he took the title from Punk. A few weeks later, Punk lost it to Undertaker. CM Punk tried repeatedly to get the title back. But Undertaker was unbeatable against Punk.

CHAPTER 5

TEAMING UP

SECOND CITY SAINTS

Punk's hometown of Chicago was the foundation for one of his first **stables**. In his years with ROH, CM Punk partnered with Colt Cabana and Ace Steel. They formed the Second City Saints in 2004.

CM Punk trained at the Steel Domain Wrestling school in Chicago. He was coached by Ace Steel. These two wrestled in tag teams together before the Second City Saints got together.

ACE STEEL

stable—a group of wrestlers who protect each other during matches and sometimes wrestle together

CM PUNK

At Steel Domain, CM Punk's training partner was Colt Cabana. They became good friends and wrestled in several tag team matches together. They also faced off against one another in ROH and in other independent wrestling leagues. Punk and Colt Cabana won two ROH Tag Team Championships in 2004.

COLT CABANA

The Second City Saints feuded against two other stables called The Prophecy and Generation Next. The team also regularly fought against Punk's enemy, Raven. Against all opponents, they had a high success rate. CM Punk left the Second City Saints in 2005 when he signed with the WWE.

STRAIGHT EDGE SOCIETY

The formation of the Straight Edge Society (SES) put CM Punk in the spotlight. Punk created the society and was its leader. Luke Gallows and Serena were the main members. SES members made statements that being clean—not using illegal drugs, alcohol, and cigarettes—put them above other wrestlers and fans. They made fun of other wrestlers, and they picked on fans who admitted to using drugs and alcohol.

NOVEMBER 2009

The SES began when the wrestler Festus decided to stop using drugs, with CM Punk's help. Along with his new lifestyle, he took the name Luke Gallows.

JANUARY 2010

Luke Gallows and CM Punk shaved the heads of audience members who wanted to join the Straight Edge Society. Serena came out of the audience and begged to be part of the SES. Punk shaved her head in front of a packed arena. In the months that followed, Serena helped in SES matches. In the first match, Gallows and Punk beat Matt Hardy and R-Truth. In the next match, John Morrison joined their opponents. But SES beat them again.

JANUARY–APRIL 2010

Others joined SES, but they didn't last long. After Triple H insulted the SES, CM Punk told him that he would become a member. The SES held him down and shaved his head. Darren Young joined the SES, but he quit when he found out that his head would be shaved.

APRIL–MAY 2010

The SES feuded with Rey Mysterio and Montel Vontavious Porter. In his match against Rey Mysterio, CM Punk had his own hair on the line. If Punk won, Rey Mysterio would join the SES. If Punk lost, Rey Mysterio would get to shave off Punk's long hair. Punk lost the match—and his hair!

The WWE ended Serena's contract. In her last match with the team, Big Show defeated the SES crew. On September 3, Gallows and Punk added Joseph Mercury to the SES and faced off against Big Show, only to be defeated again. Frustrated by Gallows' performance and his attitude, Punk delivered a G.T.S. on Gallows, officially kicking Gallows out of the SES.

JUNE - JULY 2010

The SES continued their feud with Rey Mysterio and developed a new one with Big Show.

Serena, CM Punk, and Luke Gallows said the Straight Edge Society pledge when they entered the ring at *WrestleMania* in March 2010.

With Gallows and Serena gone, the SES was done for. But CM Punk guaranteed that his message of clean living would live on.

A WINNING TAG TEAM

CM Punk and Kofi Kingston paired up for the first time in April 2008. They took control in an eight-person tag team match and won. It didn't take long for them to come out on the very top—winners of the World Tag Team title! But their quest for the title had some ups and downs.

KOFI KINGSTON

HEIGHT
6 ft (183 cm)

WEIGHT
212 lbs (96 kg)

SIGNATURE MOVE
Trouble in Paradise

FACT
Kingston excels at leaping onto opponents with high-flying moves. Punk's moves stay close to the ground. For this reason, they were great partners.

APRIL 15, 2008
Punk and Kingston won their first tag team match together. They had the help of Jimmy Wang Yang and Shannon Moore.

OCTOBER 27, 2008
CM Punk and Kingston beat Cody Rhodes and Ted DiBiase Jr. for the World Tag Team Title.

MAY 5, 2008
Punk and Kingston, along with many other ECW wrestlers, defeated Mr. Kennedy and Triple H.

SEPTEMBER 29, 2008
Punk and Kingston, along with Rey Mysterio and Evan Bourne, lost to Cody Rhodes, Ted DiBiase Jr., Kane, and Manu.

OCTOBER 7, 2008
Punk and Kingston lost to Cody Rhodes, Ted DiBiase Jr., John Morrison, and The Miz.

OCTOBER 20, 2008
John Morrison and The Miz took Punk and Kingston down again.

CHAPTER 6

CHAMPIONSHIPS

Punk has held every single WWE title. He is also a *WrestleMania* pro and has more Money in the Bank wins than most wrestlers.

WRESTLEMANIA 24

In 2008 Punk won the Money in the Bank seven-way ladder match at *WrestleMania*. He fought Carlito, Chris Jericho, John Morrison, Montel Vontavious Porter, Mr. Kennedy, and Shelton Benjamin. It was an exciting match with a lot of high-flying action. Wrestlers leaped from the ropes and from the ladder onto their opponents. Chris Jericho and CM Punk were on the ladder together when Punk trapped Jericho's leg in one of the ladder rungs. That was the final move that let CM Punk reach the briefcase at the top of the ladder and win the match.

FACT

WrestleMania started in 1985. The Money in the Bank ladder match was started at *WrestleMania* in 2005. It was part of *WrestleMania* until 2010. *SmackDown* and *Raw* now have their own Money in the Bank matches.

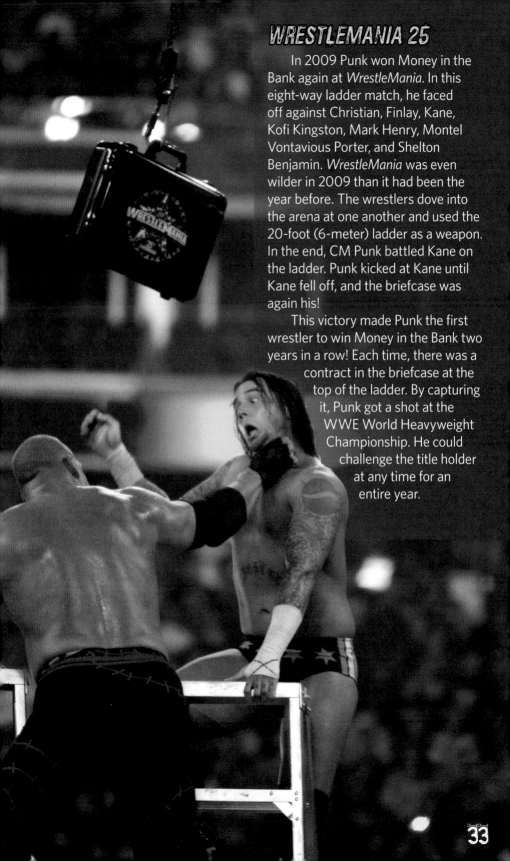

In 2009 Punk won Money in the Bank again at *WrestleMania*. In this eight-way ladder match, he faced off against Christian, Finlay, Kane, Kofi Kingston, Mark Henry, Montel Vontavious Porter, and Shelton Benjamin. *WrestleMania* was even wilder in 2009 than it had been the year before. The wrestlers dove into the arena at one another and used the 20-foot (6-meter) ladder as a weapon. In the end, CM Punk battled Kane on the ladder. Punk kicked at Kane until Kane fell off, and the briefcase was again his!

This victory made Punk the first wrestler to win Money in the Bank two years in a row! Each time, there was a contract in the briefcase at the top of the ladder. By capturing it, Punk got a shot at the WWE World Heavyweight Championship. He could challenge the title holder at any time for an entire year.

WWE WORLD
HEAVYWEIGHT CHAMPION

JUNE 30, 2008
Punk won the World Heavyweight Championship against Edge.

JULY 20, 2008
As defending champion, Punk's match against Batista ended in a **draw**.

AUGUST 17, 2008
Punk kept his championship title against JBL.

AUGUST 23, 2008
He defended it again against JBL.

SEPTEMBER 15, 2008
Punk lost his hold on the championship to Chris Jericho.

MAY 5, 2009
Punk won the championship again against Edge.

JUNE 7, 2009
Punk kept his championship against Jeff Hardy.

JUNE 15, 2009
Punk defended the championship against Jeff Hardy and Edge.

In the summer of 2008, Punk cashed in his "Money in the Bank." He defeated Edge to win the WWE World Heavyweight Championship for the first time. Punk's match against Edge was about timing. Batista had just beat up Edge during the intro of *Raw.* Suddenly CM Punk came running into the ring. Edge was lying in the ring, exhausted, and Punk used his G.T.S. on him. The championship was suddenly his.

Punk defended the championship throughout the summer. He finally lost it to Chris Jericho in September 2008. Punk fought to get it back and keep it throughout 2009.

CM Punk poses for fans wearing the World Heavyweight Championship belt.

The other ended in Punk's loss.

AUGUST 24, 2009
Punk won the championship belt back from Jeff Hardy.

AUGUST 25, 2009
Punk defended the championship against Jeff Hardy.

SEPTEMBER 13, 2009
Punk defended the championship title against Undertaker.

SEPTEMBER 22, 2009
Punk lost the WWE World Heavyweight Championship to Undertaker.

After losing the title to Chris Jericho on September 15, 2008, Punk attempted to get it back on September 30. He was unsuccessful.

draw—when a competition ends

INTERCONTINENTAL CHAMPIONSHIP

The WWE Intercontinental Championship is one of the most prestigious pro wrestling titles. But in order to win the Intercontinental title, a wrestler must win the WWE World Heavyweight title or the WWE Championship title first. CM Punk won the World Heavyweight title on June 30, 2008, so he qualified for a shot at the Intercontinental Championship.

WILLIAM REGAL

HEIGHT
6 ft, 2 in (188 cm)

WEIGHT
240 lbs (109 kg)

SIGNATURE MOVES
Regal Stench

William Regal is a wrestler many people love to hate. He's known for his arrogant attitude and flashy style. Regal wears fancy velvet robes into the ring as though he is royalty. At the end of 2008, Regal won the Intercontinental Championship. Punk was his main rival for the belt. Punk fought Regal for the title and lost. But he wasn't ready to give up.

Punk came back and defeated Regal on January 5, 2009. Regal lost through a disqualification. In a rematch, the same thing happened to Punk. Finally, a "no disqualification" match was scheduled for January 19, 2009. Punk won it, and the Intercontinental Championship was his!

Past Winners

The Intercontinental Championship has been awarded since 1979. When CM Punk won this belt, he joined a long list of big-name winners. Past winners include :

CHRIS JERICHO

REY MYSTERIO

JOHN MORRISON

JEFF HARDY

EDGE

THE TRIPLE CROWN

At the end of 2008, Punk had won the World Heavyweight Championship and the World Tag Team Championship. In order to win the Triple Crown, he had to win the Intercontinental Championship. When Punk defeated Regal for the title in January 2009, he became the 19th Triple Crown Champion in history! He even broke a record. Before him, Diesel had earned his Triple Crown in 227 days. CM Punk won the Triple Crown in only 203 days!

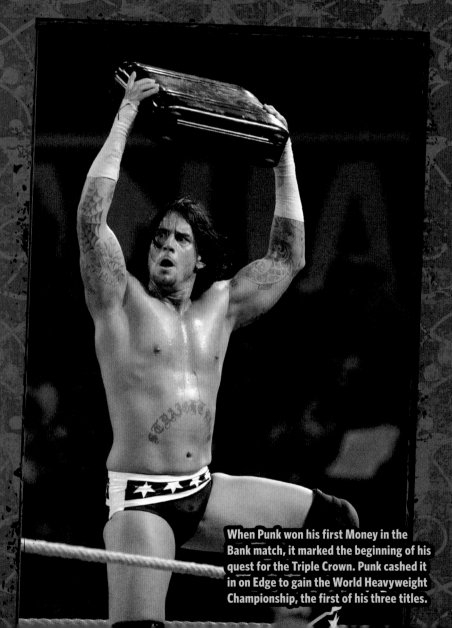

When Punk won his first Money in the Bank match, it marked the beginning of his quest for the Triple Crown. Punk cashed it in on Edge to gain the World Heavyweight Championship, the first of his three titles.

TRIPLE CROWN Winners

1. PEDRO MORALES, 1980
2. BRET HART, 1992
3. DIESEL, 1994
4. SHAWN MICHAELS, 1996
5. "STONE COLD" STEVE AUSTIN, 1998
6. THE ROCK, 1999
7. TRIPLE H, 2001
8. KANE, 2001
9. CHRIS JERICHO, 2001
10. KURT ANGLE, 2002
11. EDDIE GUERRERO, 2004
12. CHRIS BENOIT, 2004
13. RIC FLAIR, 2005
14. EDGE, 2006
15. ROB VAN DAM, 2006
16. BOOKER T, 2006
17. RANDY ORTON, 2006
18. JEFF HARDY, 2008
19. CM PUNK, 2009
20. JBL, 2009
21. REY MYSTERIO, 2009
22. THE MIZ, 2010
23. DOLPH ZIGGLER, 2011
24. CHRISTIAN, 2011
25. BIG SHOW, 2012

TRIPLE CROWN HistORY

The Triple Crown started in 1979 for what was then the WWF. At the time, the WWF Championship, the Intercontinental Championship, and the World Tag Team Championship were the only titles in the WWF. In 1997 the World Heavyweight Championship was recognized as another possible title for the Triple Crown.

FIGHT FOR THE WWE CHAMPIONSHIP

In 2011 people could not stop talking about CM Punk and John Cena. They first squared off during the WWE *Royal Rumble* in 2008. But their rivalry really heated up in 2011.

In their first WWE Championship match on July 11, 2011, Punk lost to Cena. A week later, at the Money in the Bank match on July 17, there was a lot on the line. Cena would be fired if Punk won. But Punk's contract was about to expire, and the WWE hadn't re-signed him yet.

Punk won, but Cena wasn't fired. Even worse, CM Punk's contract expired at midnight following the match. A furious Punk walked out of the stadium as the WWE Champion. A WWE Champion had never left the WWE with the championship before.

JOHN CENA

HEIGHT
6 ft, 1 in (185 cm)

WEIGHT
251 lbs (114 kg)

SIGNATURE MOVE
Attitude Adjustment

When the WWE brought CM Punk back under a new contract, there was a strange problem. Both wrestlers claimed that they held the championship title. Because Cena held it before Punk left, he felt that it was his. Obviously, Punk thought he had retained the title despite his lapsed contract. Because of this dispute the men had a rematch.

Despite their feud, CM Punk came to Cena's rescue after a September 2, 2011 match. Alberto Del Rio and Ricardo Rodriguez were ganging up on Cena until Punk came into the ring and pulled them off of Cena.

Punk won the match at *SummerSlam* on August 14. But suddenly Alberto Del Rio entered the ring and stole the title from Punk! On November 20 in *Survivor Series*, CM Punk took the championship back. He defended it again against Alberto Del Rio on November 28, 2011.

CHAPTER 7

THE FUTURE FOR PUNK

Punk's fans eagerly await his next move, both in and out of the ring. He has appeared on many TV programs. On Halloween Night 2006, Punk appeared on *Ghost Hunters Live*. On the episode, Punk helped investigate reported ghost sightings in a hotel in Colorado. Punk said that he heard the ghosts. He has also appeared on *Jimmy Kimmel Live*. He has even helped broadcast the weather report in cities where he is wrestling.

GOOD HUMOR

For 20 years the ice cream company Good Humor made WWE-themed ice cream treats. The treats were imprinted with photos of WWE star wrestlers. Good Humor quit making the ice cream treats in 2009. In the summer of 2011, Punk demanded that Good Humor bring back WWE ice cream bars—with *his* face on them! Punk's demand received a lot of fan support. If Punk and his fans keep the campaign going, there may be ice cream in WWE's future.

Delicious!

ICE CREAM

"time to chill!"

CM Punk got slimed at the 2011 Nickelodeon Kids' Choice Awards.

THE ROAD AHEAD

CM Punk has spent more than 10 years working his way up from independent wrestling leagues to becoming a WWE star. But he wants to go even farther. Punk wants to be WWE's number one superstar, and he's willing to spend years working toward that goal.

But no matter how much Punk wants to be on top, wrestling is hard on a person's body. From 2005 to 2011, CM Punk wrestled in almost 350 matches for the WWE. That comes out to almost one match a week for every week of those six years. The wear and tear resulted in some injuries. In 2010 Punk had elbow surgery, and he almost needed hip surgery.

While Punk was recovering from elbow surgery, he became a **commentator** on *Raw*. Since his recovery, Punk has been invited to be a guest commentator from time to time.

commentator—a person who calls the action at a live sporting event

Whether he's in or out of the ring, Punk knows how to entertain a crowd.

CM Punk has a lot of knowledge about wrestling and public speaking, both in and out of the ring. He provides good play-by-play information during matches. Punk is also known for being witty. He believes that good commentary makes a match even more exciting for fans. Many fans liked his work as a commentator and are hoping that he becomes a full-time commentator in the future. Punk would hate to leave the ring, but he knows that his body won't let him wrestle forever. Commentary would let him stay in the world that he loves.

GLOSSARY

babyface (BAY-bee-fayss)—a wrestler who acts as a hero in the ring

commentator (KOM-uhn-tay-ter)—a person who calls the action at a live sporting event

debut (DAY-byoo)—a first public appearance

draw (DRAW)—when a competition ends and both sides are even

finishing move (FIN-ish-ing MOOV)—the move for which a wrestler is best known; this move also is called a signature move

heel (HEEL)—a wrestler who acts as a villain in the ring

independent wrestling league (in-di-PEN-duhnt RESS-ling LEEG)—a small wrestling group that competes outside of the WWE

peer pressure (PEER PRESH-ur)—when one's friends try to get a person to do something he or she thinks is wrong

stable (STAY-buhl)—a group of wrestlers who protect each other during matches and sometimes wrestle together

steroid (STER-oid)—a drug that can increase a person's strength and athletic ability; steroids can cause heart problems and death

submission hold (suhb-MISH-uhn HOHLD)—a chokehold, joint hold, or compression lock that causes a fighter's opponent to end the match by tapping out or saying, "I submit"

tag team (TAG TEEM)—two or more wrestlers who partner together against other teams

READ MORE

Kaelberer, Angie Peterson. *The Fabulous, Freaky, Unusual History of Pro Wrestling.* Unusual Histories. Mankato, Minn.: Capstone Press, 2011.

Price, Sean. *The Kids' Guide to Pro Wrestling.* Kids' Guides. Mankato, Minn.: Capstone Press, 2012.

Raatma, Lucia. *John Cena: Rapping Wrestler with Attitude.* Pro Wrestling Stars. North Mankato, Minn.: Capstone Press, 2013.

INTERNET SITES

FactHound offers a safe, fun way to find Internet sites related to this book. All of the sites on FactHound have been researched by our staff.

Here's all you do:

Visit *www.facthound.com*

Enter this code: 9781429686938

INDEX

J
921
CM PUNK
FAN